Family Guide
To
Celebration
Of The
Jewish Holidays

Leonard and Linda Chesler

Family Guide To Celebration Of The Jewish Holidays

iUniverse books may be ordered through booksellers or by contacting:

iUniverse
1663 Liberty Drive
Bloomington, IN 47403
www.iuniverse.com
1-800-Authors (1-800-288-4677)

ISBN: 978-1-4697-3219-0 (sc)
ISBN: 978-1-4697-3220-6 (e)

Print information available on the last page.

Library of Congress Control Number: 2012900068

iUniverse rev. date: 12/17/2019

Contents

Preface

Judaism is an important part of our life and we have always tried to celebrate the Jewish Holidays together as a family. Judaism has a rich assortment of holidays and each holiday contributes to our understanding and practice of Judaism and contributes to our individual and family experience. Each holiday can also provide inspiration, insight and meaning to us as we live our daily lives.

Starting when our children were young, it soon became apparent to us that it was much better and much more meaningful if, as part of our celebration, we discussed each holiday with each other, talking about why the holiday is celebrated, its origin and history, how it is celebrated and very importantly its meaning, relevance and value to us today and what we can learn and use in our everyday lives.

We wanted our children to feel and understand that the holidays and their Judaism were important for them and each holiday had meaning and value for them and should be celebrated by them for its own sake, not just because they wanted to please their parents and grandparents.

Over time we wrote up these discussions and added information for each holiday for our family use. At the urging of many family members and friends who have since seen and liked this material, we would now like to share it and make it also available for others to use.

In the following chapters each holiday is discussed in terms of an Introduction Section, Celebration Section, and Theme. The Introduction Section presents an overview discussion of the holiday and its history and background.

The Celebration section discusses how the holiday is celebrated. The Theme Section presents a concluding summary and points of interest with emphasis placed on purpose, meaning, value, Joy and inspiration for each holiday and use in our daily lives.

We feel confident that the reader will find this material as valuable and useful as we have, for our own family and friends, in helping to celebrate the Jewish Holidays.

Introduction

Starting over 4000 years ago with our forefathers, Abraham, Isaac and Jacob, our Jewish ideals and traditions were developed based on the concept of a universal God that is good and just.

Human life and everything else were sanctified by God's creation and each of us was blessed with the right to life and the ability, along with God's help, to participate in and continue with the process of creation, a loving process of righteousness in which along with God's help we care for and take care of ourselves, care for and take care of each other and care for and try to improve the world and everything in it. We achieve this love and caring through righteous behavior and we observe and honor this sanctity in everything that we do.

Consistent with this belief and toward this purpose, Jewish traditions, customs, principles and methods of individual and community religious practice and daily study were established and developed, based on the experience of thousands of years, to help each of us as individuals and to help each of us together as a community to better practice and apply these concepts in our everyday lives to in turn help us to obtain fulfillment and achieve our full potential as human beings.

These developed traditions and religious practices include prayer, study and discussion with other members of the community at the synagogue or temple as well as celebrations and social activities at the synagogue or temple and prayer, and study and religious practice on an individual basis with our families and friends at our homes and in our communities.

An extensive heritage of written and oral Jewish knowledge has been developed, including the Ten Commandments and the Torah of Moses (the first 5 books of the Bible), the Haftarah (Prophets in the Bible), the remainder of the Bible (Writings), the Talmud, the Midrash, subsequent Jewish teachings, principles and discussions and our modern prayer books (Siddurs for daily prayer and the festivals, Mahzors for Rosh Hashanah and Yom Kippur and Haggadahs for Passover) and our modern Rabbi's teachings and writings.

At the temple or synagogue we participate with other members of the community in prayer, reading, studying and discussing the Torah, Haftarah and appropriate material from our other extensive Jewish written and oral heritage and how this applies to our own situation and the situation of our family, friends and our community.

Our tradition requires study and learning on an ongoing basis to understand how to best apply these concepts of righteousness to our daily lives.

It is not enough that we want to be righteous; we must also be willing to study, learn and understand our situation so that the outcomes of what we do will accomplish our righteous goal of "doing the right thing." Our traditions, customs, prayers and religious ideals help us do this, as well as help us find self value and inspiration on an ongoing basis.

Celebration of our Jewish Holidays and festivals is an important part of this process. Holidays become an important time for being with family and friends, an important time for reflection and understanding and in many cases an important time for joyous celebration, and for all of these reasons can have a significant positive impact on our lives.

Holidays and Festivals

We have a variety of holidays and each has its own story to tell. Each has its own focus, meaning and value for us as we go through the year.

Each presents its own situation, facts and ideas to give us insight on different aspects of our lives. Each holiday is an opportunity to gain insight and strengthen our feelings of self value, caring and love and a chance to share these feelings with our family, friends and the community.

The following Chapters discuss each holiday in more detail. For each holiday there is an Introduction Section, Celebration Section and Theme.

An overview and background discussion are presented in the Introduction. The Celebration Section presents information on how the holiday is celebrated, and a concluding summary and points of emphasis are presented in the Theme Section.

In the Jewish calendar, the day begins at sunset. So for example, the Sabbath, the seventh day of the week, begins on Friday evening at sunset and ends on Saturday at sunset. All holidays begin at sunset of the day before.

The Jewish calendar has 12 months. Months are lunar months with 29 or 30 days. With an average month length of 29 ½ days and with 12 months, there are only 354 days in the year. To keep the calendar consistent with the seasons and the years which correspond to the earth's rotation around the sun, an extra month was added to the calendar seven times every nineteen years.

A special blessing for the new month is made at the temple or synagogue on the first day (Rosh Hodesh) of the new month and on the Sabbath before the beginning of the month.

A more detailed discussion of the Jewish calendar is presented in the Appendix which also discusses the Internet as an additional source of information on food, songs/music, and ways to celebrate.

Sabbath

Introduction

The Sabbath (in Hebrew called Shabbat, which is related to the verb shavat, cease, desist, rest (Ref. 1, Volume 14, page 558) is observed every week, starting on sundown, Friday Evening and ending after sundown on Saturday, the next day, and is a day of peace and rest.

The Sabbath in addition to being a day of physical rest, is also a day of emotional and spiritual peace and renewal.

In Genesis, in the Torah, it is mentioned that God worked six days in creating the world, but on the 7th day God stopped working and declared the 7th day holy.

To make sure the Sabbath is observed, we are further commanded in the Ten Commandments, in the Torah, in which the Fourth Commandment says in part:

"Remember the Sabbath Day to keep it holy."

"Six days shalt thou labor, and do all thy work."
"But the seventh day is the Sabbath of the Lord thy God: in it thou shalt not do any work, thou, nor thy son, nor thy daughter, thy manservant, nor thy maidservant, nor thy cattle, nor thy stranger that is within thy gates." (Ref. 2, page12)

This shows us that God cares about us, cares about our well-being and in fact cares about every one and, as part of creation, God wants us to also care about ourselves and each of us to care about each other.

In other words the Sabbath is to be treated as a universal holy day, celebrating and commemorating creation, and through this celebration and commemoration, indicating to us the importance and sanctity of what has been created including the importance, sanctity, and holiness of our own lives, everyone else's lives, and the world in which we live.

On the Sabbath we remind ourselves that we are not to treat ourselves and each other as though we were just a collection of mindless machines without feelings or meaning beyond the value of the work we produce.

In God's eyes each of us is special and holy and, on the Sabbath, God has given us a chance to recognize this.

We have been given a chance to rest from work and our normal activities, to appreciate and celebrate the beauty, value, meaning and love that is within us and in the rest of the world.

We have been given the chance to understand the importance and value of doing our best to appreciate and value life and to, properly, take care of what we have been given and the joy and peace that this can bring.

Celebration

Once a week, the Sabbath becomes a day of rest, relaxation, prayer, study, song, feasting, celebration and peace. The Sabbath becomes a day when we take time off from our daily work and from dealing with the everyday necessities of our lives.

We have time to contemplate our own feelings about things, to be with our families and friends, and to be with and participate with other members of the community in services at the temple or synagogue.

On Friday evening, at home before sunset, candles are lit to commemorate the beginning of the Sabbath.

Typically by tradition, the candles are lit by the women (if available) in the house who also recite the following blessing:

"Ba-ruch A-ta Adonni, E-lo-hey-nu Me-lech ha-o-lam a-sher ki-d'-sha-nu b'mitz-vo-tav v'tzi-vanu l'hadlik ner shel Shabbat (English pronunciation of the Hebrew version of the prayer)."

"Blessed are you, Lord our God, King of the universe who has sanctified us through your commandments and who has commanded us to light the candles on the Sabbath."

In many homes, additional blessings and personal prayers are also recited.

This could include for example, a traditional blessing for the entire family, recited by the head of the household, "May the Lord bless you and keep you. May the Lord cause his countenance to shine upon you and be gracious unto you. May the Lord lift up his countenance toward you and grant you peace." (Reference 5, page 188)

The candles, their lighting, and the blessings and prayers recited over them have become a symbol of the light, life, love and hope that we pray for and want for ourselves and the rest of the world.

Each week the beginning of the Sabbath ushers in a special time for us to rest from our daily concerns, to study and contemplate, to be together with family and friends, sharing and enjoying ourselves and each other, giving us personal feelings and memories of happiness, fulfillment and self worth.

Traditionally the Sabbath Evening meal is treated as a special meal in the week. Before beginning, the Kiddush, a blessing for the wine and the Sabbath, is recited and then a blessing for the Chalah, the traditional braided Sabbath bread, is recited. Either a fish or meat course or both are served.

In the temple or synagogue on Friday Evening and Saturday, in addition to the regular daily prayer service, prayers to honor the Sabbath are recited. In the Saturday Sabbath service, a Torah portion and corresponding Haftarah (conclusion) portion from the Prophets section of the Bible are read.

The Saturday Sabbath service is also the time that boys and girls celebrating their Bar and Bat Mitzvahs are honored by participating in the Sabbath services and reading portions of the Torah and Haftarah.

Traditionally work and normal week-day activities are not performed or are minimized on the Sabbath. For example many people prepare meals on Friday, ahead of time for the Sabbath, and do not cook or perform other chores on the Sabbath and many will walk to temple/synagogue and other places rather than drive if possible.

The Sabbath has been honored throughout our history.

It has always been considered that every person must, no matter what their stature or position, personally participate in preparing for, observing and honoring the Sabbath.
Thus, there are many stories of famous Jewish Scholars who would make sure that they personally did some special work (e. g.,

preparing food, cleaning, etc.) to prepare for the Sabbath, even if they had others normally available to do these kinds of things for them.

The idea is that the Sabbath is for each of us and when we personally get involved, participate and deal with it, we get the most out of it.

The Sabbath is a time for happiness and relaxation. Traditional songs sung with meals called Z'mirot express the joy of the Sabbath. One of the most well known Zimirot is called Koh Robbon Olam, which is chanted on Friday evening and describes the wonders of God's creation.

As previously mentioned, in the Temple or Synagogue, on the Sabbath, a portion (Sidra) of the Torah is read (There are also Torah readings on new moon, holiday and fast-day afternoon services). Members of the congregations are honored by being called up to the reading (this act is referred as an Aliyah).

After concluding reading from the Torah, a section from the Prophets part of the Bible, called the Haftarah (or conclusion) is read. Each portion of the Torah has its own specific Haftarah which are related by some common theme. Some Sabbath days are named after the Haftarah reading.

After the Sabbath Day (Saturday) service, it has become the practice, referred to as Oneg Shabbat ("Sabbath Joy", originally attributed to the modern Hebrew poet, Hayyim Nahman Bialik, Reference 2 page 17), in many temples and synagogues for the congregation to gather together for discussion refreshments and songs.

A special blessing for the new month is made at the temple or synagogue on the first day (Rosh Hodash) of the new month and on the Sabbath before the beginning of the month.

Theme

God created the world. We are part of that creation and were given life. So on the Sabbath we celebrate this creation, we celebrate the creation of the world and life and are grateful for our own life and the sanctity and holiness God has given to each of us.

By setting aside a special day of rest from normal daily activities, God shows us the sanctity and holiness of what was created.

We are not just automata, elaborate mechanisms exercising the laws of nature, inexorably moving from one state to the next, but rather we exist at a higher level where we can, along with God's help, share in and continue the process of creation for righteous purpose.

In nature there is no day of rest, everything competes, there is constant conflict and struggle and there is no peace.

But as human beings God has given us the ability, that with knowledge and understanding, we can rise above these issues and create through righteous behavior a more hopeful, loving, caring, joyous, humane and meaningful life.

Once a week on the Sabbath we recognize this, and this also then gives us a chance to apply these same feelings of hope, sanctity, caring, love and righteousness to our daily activities the rest of the week, helping us to do our best to give our life meaningfulness, usefulness and value.

Passover (Pesach)

Introduction

On Passover we remember a time period over three thousand years ago when we were enslaved in the land of Egypt and we remember how we were delivered by God to freedom and given our Jewish ideals and way of life to help maintain and continue that freedom.

We identify with the past to better appreciate the value of freedom and liberty not only for ourselves but for all mankind. Passover calls upon us to do all that we can to remove all forms of tyranny and bondage.

On Passover, through our prayers, rituals, symbols and songs we think of our selves as though we were slaves and then given freedom. We celebrate our liberation and dedicate ourselves to our Jewish values and way of life as a way to preserve and continue this freedom, for ourselves and everyone else, and work toward relinquishing all forms of tyranny and injustice.

We want, for ourselves and all mankind, that we be free from oppression, free from want, free in mind and spirit, and free to develop all the gifts which God has given to each of us.

Passover is also a holiday that coincides with spring, and the concept of renewal that takes place in nature at this time of year is also included in the Passover Celebration. In ancient times renewal took place as a time for planting new crops and preparing for the year ahead. In our time, the message of Passover can also give us hope, inspiration and a spirit of renewal for dealing with our life in the coming year.

Based on the Jewish calendar (a lunar calendar with each month generally being 29 or 30 days), Passover begins at sundown on the 14th day of the Jewish month of Nisan. This generally corresponds to the end of March or the beginning or middle of April. Passover lasts eight days (traditionally seven days in Israel) and ends eight days later at sundown on the 22nd day of Nisan.

Celebration

The first night is celebrated in the home with an evening observance called a Seder. Many Ashkenazi Jews also have a second Seder celebration on the second night. The Seder is a religious observance in which we retell the story of how we were freed from slavery in Egypt and praise God as the source of all life and liberty. The Seder service follows the text of the Haggadah which is the prayer book used for the Seder.

Over the years there have been many versions of Haggadahs prepared for the Seder service. Each family should choose the Haggadah version with which they are most comfortable.

Generally the Haggadah presents instruction on how to conduct the Seder service the Seder meal, discussion of the holiday, the meaning and purpose of each of the items covered in the service, prayers for the service, and stories, discussion and songs to help each member of the family participate in and get the most from the Passover celebration.

For many, preparation before the start of the Holiday and the Seder can include cleaning the house of all crumbs of bread (Hametz) and preparing separate plates and utensils specifically reserved for use on Passover.

Seder is a Hebrew word which means order. The order of the

Seder and the content of what is done are depicted in the text of the Haggadah.

Before the start of the Seder, the table is set with a Ceremonial Seder Plate, containing Bayzah (roasted or hard boiled egg), Maror (bitter herb, usually horseradish), Z'roa (shank bone or roasted meat bone, symbol of the paschal lamb), Haroset (nuts, apples, cinnamon, and wine) and Karpas (green vegetable -- celery, parsley, etc. to be dipped in the salt water). Also placed on the table is a plate containing three pieces of matzah (covered), a dish with salt water, and a decanter of wine. As will be discussed, each of these items has symbolic significance and use in the service.

The Seder starts with the blessing of the first cup of wine, sanctifying the name of God and proclaiming the holiness of the Passover festival.

A blessing is made over a green vegetable (Karpas) to express our thankfulness for springtime and natures renewal and we renew our own hope and faith for freedom, justice and a better world. Before the blessing, the Karpas is dipped into salt water. It is said, to remind us of the tears the oppressed Israelites shed before they were liberated.

Earlier a plate with three pieces of matzah had been placed on the table. The three pieces represent the three classifications of Jews in ancient Judea (the upper one Khoen, which were the high priests during the time of the temple, the middle Levi, which were the workers in the temple, and the third Yisrael , which were the rest of the people). During the Seder everyone will eat from all three Matzot to illustrate that all Jews are united in a covenant of equality.

The middle piece of matzah is broken into two Pieces, the smaller is put back to be used for a later blessing. The larger piece is wrapped in a napkin as a symbol of unleavened dough. It will be eaten as the Afikoman at the end of the meal.

The service then focuses on the story of Passover. How it came about that the Jews became enslaved in the land of Egypt. Their work and lives were bitter and harsh. How Moses was selected by God to go to Pharaoh (the Egyptian ruler) and ask that the Jews be freed.

Pharaoh and the Egyptians refused to release the Jews from slavery. Then a series of ten plagues were brought against the Egyptians before they finally agreed to let the Jews go.

The Jews had to leave Egypt quickly but were blocked by the Red Sea. In the meantime Pharaoh changed his mind about letting the Jews go and sent his army to pursue the Jews.

God split the Sea so that the Jews could get to the other side, but when the Egyptian Army tried to follow the Jews across where the water had been split, they, the Egyptian Army, were destroyed by the waters coming back together upon them.

Once free from the Egyptians, we were given, at Mt. Sinai, the Ten Commandments and Torah as the basis for how we should, in a righteous and moral way, treat ourselves, treat each other and live together.

This basis for living was very important then as it is now. The Jews had been slaves for so long they were not used to making their own decisions, taking responsibility, or making moral choices. This Jewish way of life was able to give them inspiration, hope and courage as it can also do for us today.

The story of our freedom and exodus is told and discussed by the whole family. The children ask and sing the four questions which discuss the basic question "Why is this night different from all other nights?"

We are told that we eat matzah because when our ancestors were told they could leave Egypt they had no time to bake bread with leaven to make it rise in the normal way and they had to bake it without leaven.

At the Seder we eat bitter herbs to remind us of the bitterness of our ancestors' slavery. We also remind ourselves of this bitterness by dipping food twice in salt water and dipping food in haroset which represents the bricks and mortar of their harsh labor.

The concept of how to tell the story of the exodus is then discussed in the context of telling the story to four types of children, each with different levels of experience, maturity and point of view. This is done to show how important it is that there be adequate discussion and communication at the Seder of the significance and importance of the Passover Holiday and its message for all of us today.

The Haggadah discusses the plagues brought on the Egyptians until they finally relented and let the Jewish people go. The point is made that we can not fully rejoice and celebrate our freedom when we know that our freedom involved the suffering of the Egyptians.

We cannot be joyous when any human being is afflicted, even an enemy. As a result, in the service, as we mention each of the 10 plagues we spill some wine from the second cup of wine. Our second cup of wine, as a symbol of our gladness, is diminished by the wine we spilled to express sorrow for the Egyptians.

In the more general sense, the sorrow of course is that, had the message of Passover been understood and followed, there wouldn't have been slaves and their task masters wouldn't have had to be defeated and much needless suffering and wasting would have been averted.

The Seder continues with the hymn of thanksgiving "Dayyenu". Dayyenu begins with "How thankful we should be to God, for his many deeds of kindness for us!" The Hymn then proceeds to list the series of things that God did for us at the time of the exodus. After each item is mentioned, we say "Dayyenu". Which means, "it would have been sufficient" to that point, had not the additional things been performed.

The list of God's deeds, for which we are thankful, starts with being freed by the Egyptians and ends with being given the Torah and our Jewish way of life to help us maintain our freedom and all our gifts of humanity.

The importance of explaining the significance of the symbols of the Pascal lamb, unleavened bread, and bitter herb is emphasized, at this point in the service, where the significance of each one is questioned and then explained (Many Haggadahs quote Rabbi Gamaliel (grandson of the great sage Hillel) as saying: "He who has not explained the following symbols of the Seder has not fulfilled his duty: Pesah, the Pascal Lamb; Matzah, the unleavened Bread; Maror, the bitter herb.").

The service then continues to the Blessing and drinking of the second cup of wine, the blessing for washing our hands and the blessing for the matzah and bitter herb. After this, the table is cleared and the Seder meal is begun.

 After the Seder meal is finished, the tradition is that the Seder meal cannot be completed without eating the Afikoman (the middle piece of matzah that was hidden earlier) which is our modern substitute for the Paschal Lamb which, years ago, was the final food of the Seder feast.

So after the Seder meal is completed, the Host or Leader asks for the Afikoman. Previously it was hidden and the children (and grown up children also) had fun looking for it. Finally it is produced, but not before some type of "reward " is given for its receipt, and the Host or Leader gives a sigh of relief (because the service can not go on without it). The idea is for everyone to have some fun at this point in the service.

The Seder service then continues with prayers of thankfulness for the food we have eaten, for the blessings of our Torah and Jewish Traditions and we pray for the future of our family friends, community and the coming of the messianic era.

In the tradition of the Seder Service, the Haggadah contains the message "all who are hungry come and eat" and among the awaited guests is the Prophet Elijah.

In Jewish legend, Elijah is the champion of the oppressed, he brings hope and relief to the downtrodden, and performs miracles of rescue. He is associated with the bringing of good tidings, joy and peace.

There is the legend that Elijah appears at every Seder and sips some wine from a cup especially prepared for him.

At this point in the Seder, the cup of wine for Elijah is prepared, we open the door and rise in the hope that Elijah will come in and we say "Baruh Habah" (Blessed Be He Who Comes) and as we sing the song of Elijah in the Haggadah, we pray that we will soon see fulfilled Elijah's hope and our hope for a world of freedom and peace for all mankind.

Like Elijah, despite the sad state of affairs and problems in the world, we still maintain our faith and work towards a world of freedom and peace for all mankind.

The Seder then continues with prayers and songs of thankfulness that the whole family can participate in. The blessing is made over the 4th cup of wine and then there are concluding prayers and hymns.

Theme

A basic idea of Passover is freedom: Freedom with responsibility, to take care of ourselves and to take care of each other; Freedom maintained by our Jewish righteous way of life; A way of life to protect us, inspire us and let us grow and develop to our full, God given, human potential.

Freedom starts with an idea, the idea that each of us is special, that each of us is important, that each of us has something to offer the world.

This realization gives us conviction and strength to break the bonds that contain the spirit, to dispel feelings of hopelessness and despair, and gives us the courage to work, to go on and deal with the things that limit ourselves whether they be physical, emotional, intellectual, economic, social or political.

As part of this, we must also learn to break the bonds that limit our thinking to only ourselves. The more we get involved beyond ourselves, the more significant and broader we become.
We must work to take care of ourselves and satisfy our own needs. But if we only think of ourselves, we will never be free of these needs. We will always be slaves.

However, by broadening our lives we break these shackles. We must all try in our own way to make others feel love, compassion and caring. By becoming part of the process of making this a better place - a more humane and plentiful world, we also enrich and give more meaning to our own lives.

Our forefathers were slaves and lacked courage to be free. Then they found that courage, in the Sinai Desert, by choosing to follow the ways that God had given them, our Jewish heritage and traditions, ways to help build a more humane world.

The life we lead builds the house within which our spirit dwells.

Today on Passover, just as our forefathers - we too must choose: Will we place our spirit in a house built in the desert, barren of life, love, caring and future hope or,

will we exercise our freedom to choose to live in the house of the Lord;

a place where our spirits are warmed in the winters of our lives and cooled in our summers; a place where our hearts can play and delight in the beauties and wonders of life; a place from which we gain solace, protection and peace - forever.

Shavuot

Introduction

As discussed on Passover, we were not only delivered from slavery but we were also blessed with the gift of Torah and our Jewish way of life, as the moral and righteous way to live together and maintain that freedom.

On Shavuot, we celebrate this wonderful gift, the receipt of the Torah on Mount Sinai. Shavuot means weeks and it follows exactly seven weeks after the second day of Passover on the sixth and seventh days of the Hebrew month of Sivan (approximately at the end of May or beginning of June).

Shavuot is also referred to as the festival of the giving of the law ("Z'man Matan Toratenu") refering to the Ten Commandments which God gave to Mosses on Mount Sinai and which are part of the Torah.

We are all familiar with these commandments; not to murder, not to steal, not to bare false witness, to maintain one's sanctity and the sanctity of family and home, and not to worship idols or false Gods or use the name of God in vain.

These commandments were made for everyone. They were given to protect and give value to each person, and they show how important and sanctified each person's life is in the eyes of God.

God is equally caring and concerned about each of us. No one is entitled to more or less justice, fairness, mercy or love and these points form the basis for Jewish moral and ethical thought.

Along these lines, Hillel, a famous Jewish Rabbi and scholar who lived more than two thousand years ago, said that the essence of Torah was to not do anything to anyone else that would be distasteful to you.

He said the rest is commentary and we should study on how to apply this, on an ongoing basis to our everyday lives.

In other words, we should treat each other, the way we want to be treated, in a good righteous, positive way, with fairness, justice and caring, and when we treat each other in this way we can live together and work together, as individuals and as a society, toward reaching everyone's full potential for happiness and success.

So on Shavuot we celebrate and are grateful to God for giving us this wonderful gift, a way of life that allowed us then, and allows us now, to live together and maintain our freedom on an ongoing basis, after being delivered from slavery.

In ancient times Shavuot also corresponded to a Harvest time (for example the harvest of wheat and the ripening of fruit) which adds to the tradition and celebration of the holiday.

It is appropriate that as we celebrate the harvest of crops and renewal in spring we also celebrate the moral renewal resulting from receipt of the Torah on Mount Sinai, giving us a way to maintain our freedom and live together in a loving righteous and caring way, treating each other with dignity, respect and peace.

Celebration

At the temple or synagogue, special prayer services for Shavuot are recited. In addition to the regular holiday services, the Book of Ruth is read. King David was descended from Ruth and this story of devotion and faith, which took place in ancient times during the Shavuot harvest period, has become part of the tradition of the Shavuot celebration.

During the Shavuot service, the Akdamut Prayer is chanted which praises God and thanks God for giving us the Torah. This Hymn has a distinct melody which has, over the years, become as associated with Shavuot as the famous Kol Nidre prayer has become associated with Yom Kippur.

It is customary to decorate the temple or synagogue and homes with plants and flowers to celebrate the harvest nature of the holiday. The custom has also developed of eating dairy foods on Shavuot such as cheese blintzes (type of cooked dough wrapped around cheese), cheese cake, and other dairy delicacies. Eating dairy has variously been explained as symbolizing comparing the Torah with the delight of milk and honey and that at the time the Torah was first received on the Sabbath, no meat could be properly prepared till after the Sabbath, so dairy was eaten.

A newer custom has also developed where many youngsters who have completed their course of religious studies also celebrate confirmation or graduation services at this time. This is consistent with our traditional emphasis on the importance of study and learning, as a way to help better understand and apply Torah and our Jewish ideals to our daily lives.

Theme

On Shavuot we remember back to a time thousands of years ago when, after being delivered by God from slavery in Egypt, we were then also given the gift of Torah on Mount Sinai as the basis of how, protected by a moral and righteous way of life, we could live together, as individuals and a society, and flourish while maintaining that freedom.

History tells us, that when people are not governed by individual moral and ethical behavior, society, in order to exist, will inevitably impose constraints and controls that destroy individual opportunity and freedom.

In order to live and work together we must be able to get along with each other. We can't get along with each other and we can't live together in a free society if we don't value each other, treat each other with dignity and respect and can't trust each other not to lie, steal or, worst of all, destroy and kill each other.

These actions of course were prohibited by the Ten Commandments, the Torah and the subsequent development of our Jewish way of life. The basic idea is that when we all work together and respect each other we can do much more, we can accomplish much more and we can be much happier.

The Ten Commandments and the Torah were for everyone. God cares about each of us. No one should be treated unjustly or unfairly.

As discussed earlier, this was summarized by Hillel over two thousand years ago when he said that the essence of Torah was to not do anything to anyone else that would be distasteful to you.

This tells us that we should all treat each other the way we all want to be treated and we will all be able to work together in dealing with life's ongoing issues. We must recognize and treat each other as human beings with the same types of feelings and rights that we have.

With this as a basis, our ancestors were able to develop our Jewish moral and ethical way of life.

On Shavuot we celebrate and give thanks for this way of life. We celebrate that we were given this chance, starting with receipt of the Ten Commandments and Torah on Mount Sinai, to be able to live together, work together and honor and care for each other while achieving fulfillment as individuals and a society.

So as we remember Mount Sinai, the receipt of the Torah, the Ten Commandments and the subsequent development of our Jewish Ideals, we understand and appreciate the wonderful gift we have been given, of the ability to be able to live together and take care of each other, and we know and understand the importance and value, of studying, interpreting and applying these ideals on an ongoing basis to our daily lives.

Rosh Hashanah and Yom Kippur

Introduction

The Jewish New Year starts with the holidays of Rosh Hashanah and Yom Kippur.

Rosh Hashanah is the first two days of the New Year and starts on the 1st day of the Jewish month of Tishri. Yom Kippur occurs ten days later on the 10th of Tishri. Both holidays start on the previous evening (generally Rosh Hashanah begins in September and Yom Kippur begins in September or the beginning of October).

This ten day period from the beginning of Rosh Hashanah to the end of Yom Kippur is referred to as the High Holy Days. As they start the beginning of the New Year, the High Holy Days are an important time for reflection, prayer and self renewal.

On Rosh Hashanah and Yom Kippur we go to temple or synagogue where we pray with other members of the congregation and reflect on the past year. We reflect on how we can improve on the things that we do for ourselves, our family, our friends, our community, our country and the world and we pray with the congregation for a good and happy new year.

We believe that we have been given the gift of life and as part of this gift have been given the ability to participate, along with God's help, in the process of creation. We believe that this should be a process of righteousness in which along with God's help we care for and take care of ourselves, our family, our friends, and our community and we try to improve the world and everything in it.

But all year we have been busy with our lives; working on obtaining the income and the things we need to live. We have had to deal with our family, friends and community. We had to deal with business and personal issues. We have had to deal with concerns about national and global issues which could have potential impacts on our lives.

We also have tried to have fun and enjoy ourselves. We all want to be successful, get recognition, satisfy our interests, be healthy, find love, protect the people and things we care about and obtain fulfillment and meaning for our lives.

While we have been busy all year dealing with these issues, we may now not be happy with what has actually happened. We may be concerned about mistakes or question the wisdom or correctness of our priorities, choices and behavior.

We may feel that we didn't always do our best or act toward our best wishes. For, in spite of our efforts and because of things beyond our control, we may not have done or achieved what we wanted for ourselves or the people and things we care about and we may now still have concerns about the future.

But the High Holidays, at the beginning of the New Year, starting with Rosh Hashanah and going through Yom Kippur gives us, each year, another chance for renewal and change.

With self reflection, a sincere desire for follow-up righteous change and the actual implementation of these improvements along with prayer for God's help, we renew our hope for the coming year and for our participation in and the achievement of a better world.

We believe that Rosh Hashanah and Yom Kippur, at the beginning of the New Year, celebrate the birthday of the world, the birthday of creation. We believe that creation is an ongoing process and that we have been blessed with the ability to participate in and along with God's help, make righteous contributions to this process.

God wants us to succeed in this endeavor. Thus, on the High Holidays we are given a chance to be evaluated and judged by God and ourselves and improve.

During this period we look back at our behavior for the previous year and along with God judge what we have done and how we can do better. We renew our determination to change the things in our own behavior that have been lacking. We renew our hope and pray for God's help for a good year.

Celebration

We celebrate Rosh Hashanah and Yom Kippur with temple or synagogue services and discussion and reflection at home. Services are attended on Rosh Hashanah (including the evening before) and Yom Kippur (including the evening before).

The services follow the text of the Mahzor, for Rosh Hashanah and Yom Kippur, which is the prayer book used for Rosh Hashanah and Yom Kippur. In addition to the Mahzor, the Torah and Haftarah portions that fall on Rosh Hashanah and Yom Kippur are also read and discussed.

The services focus on self analysis, judgment, prayer and the need for righteous improvement. The service follows the idea that there is a Book of Life in which each individual's words, deeds and thoughts over the past year are recorded and are now available for God's evaluation and judgment.

But God wants us to succeed and the evaluation and judgment are to motivate us, move us and give us another chance to improve. God wants us to take responsibility, to do the best we can, to reach our full potential for love, caring, righteous behavior and contribution to making the world better and achieve the resulting fulfillment that this will bring.

We believe that everyone no matter who we are or what we have or have not achieved should now make changes to improve themselves, in this regard, in the new year.

Therefore in the service the Mahzor emphasizes "Penitence, Prayer and Righteous Deeds ("U-t'shuvah u-t'fillah u-tz'dakah") as the way to achieve what is required.

We must recognize and understand the things in our feelings, actions and behavior that should be changed and improved. We then pray for God's guidance and help to achieve the required changes and we must subsequently take all of the actions necessary to actually, in fact, implement the changes and achieve the desired results.

We believe that God always gives us the opportunity and that we always have the opportunity to change and improve to achieve a more meaningful and fulfilling life.

This is further illustrated by a story (Ref. 2.) that is told about an angel who did some wrongdoing and to redeem himself was sent to earth and asked to find the most precious thing there.

The angel found one situation after another where people acted righteously to help others even to the point of sacrificing their own lives for others. The angel was told that all of these things were very precious but were not considered to be the most precious and he was sent back to continue his search.

Desperately the angel flew in every direction wondering what he could find that would be more precious than what he had already found. Suddenly something caught his eye and he swooped down just as a criminal was about to kill an innocent man.

At the last moment the criminal felt sorry for his victim. The criminal repented and did not do the terrible deed. As he watched the man struggling in his grasp, the attacker blinked and a tear rolled down his cheek. The angel scooped up the tear and brought it back to Heaven.

The tear of repentance was the most precious thing on earth and the angel was forgiven and was once more accepted in heaven.

During the Rosh Hashanah and Yom Kippur services the Shofar (horn) is blown as part of the service observance (if the first day of Rosh Hashanah lands on the Sabbath, the Shofar is not blown until the second day).

The Shofar, usually made out of a rams horn (technically it could also be made out of any clean (Kosher) animal's horn except a cow or an ox), dates back to biblical times when it was sounded to herald great events or as signal or warning to the community.

The Shofar is blown during the services to act as a "wake up call" to the congregation. The sounds of the Shofar emphasize the importance and seriousness of the service and the need for the spirit of renewal and change that the service presents.

The 10 day High Holiday period starts with services on the first two days of Rosh Hashanah and concludes with services on Yom Kippur.

After services on Rosh Hashanah we gather with family and friends for a festive meal and wish each other a happy, healthy and joyous year. We do the same when we break the fast at the conclusion of services on Yom Kippur.

Before Rosh Hashanah greeting cards are sent with the wish "May you be inscribed for a good and happy year" ("L'Shanah Tovah Tikatevu!").

On the afternoon of the first day of Rosh Hashanah (or second day if the first is a Sabbath) many Jews follow the tradition of gathering on the shore of a flowing body of water and casting crumbs of bread, symbolic of sins and broken promises, into the flowing water. This is referred to as Tashlich which means "you will cast" which is another form of atonement and contributes to atonement and cleansing for the new year.

Yom Kippor services are held the evening before the day of Yom Kippur and start again the next day and last until evening.

On the day before Yom Kippur, in the late afternoon, we eat the meal that precedes the fast of Yom Kippur. This meal must be eaten before sunset. After that we fast until after sunset on the following day.

We do not fast to punish ourselves or to feel discomfort or pain. We fast as a chance to demonstrate to ourselves, through the symbolic act of fasting, that we have the strength, determination and resolve to do the things necessary to achieve the changes and improvements required by the service.

It is the spirit of the fast that counts. Fasting is just another way for us to emphasize to ourselves the importance of what we have to do and to demonstrate to ourselves and reinforce for ourselves that we have the conviction, dedication and strength to do what will be required.

If someone can not fast because of health or physical problems they still can have the resolve, conviction and spirit to accomplish what is required. Anyone who is sick, has health problems, or feels discomfort should not fast. Children under thirteen should not fast.

The service in the evening before Yom Kippur day includes the famous KoL Nidre prayer. Kol means "all" and "Nidre" means vows. It refers to times in our history when we were subjected to persecution and were not able to openly practice our religion and beliefs.

An example of this was the Inquisition in fifteenth century Spain and Portugal where Jews were forced in many cases to give up their faith and had to practice their Jewish religion in secret (These Jews are referred to as Marranos. There are many interesting books written about these Jews, their descendants and this time in history.).

In Kol Nidre we beg God to forgive us for any false oaths, not carried out, made under pressure and severe circumstances. Kol Nidre refers only to vows made by man to God. Other vows and promises that are made, to each other or in our activities and in our daily lives cannot be negated or done away with by reciting a prayer.

On Yom Kippur, the service includes recital of the Yizkor memorial service for any family members, loved ones and friends, members of the community and all others who have unfortunately passed away.

This prayer service gives us a chance to pay tribute to those who we love, to thank God for the chance to have known and shared our lives with them, and we pray that God will take care of them and protect them, and continue to keep their love and memory in our hearts as a source of ongoing support and inspiration, and we acknowledge the greatness and universality of God who sanctifies and gives meaning to all human life, including our own.

Also on Yom Kippur the Book of Jonah Portion of the Haftarah (Prophets Portion of the Bible) is read. It describes the well known story of Jonah, who is asked by God to go to the biblical city of Ninevah and tell the people there to repent and change or they will be destroyed by their evil ways.

Jonah objects and does not want to go and tell them to repent and change, because he says that they have been too evil to be saved and, even if they now repent and sincerely change, they do not deserve forgiveness even though this would be God's wish.

So he does not want to go. He defies God and try's to run away on a ship. The ship is threatened by a severe storm which Jonah knows is the result of his defiance of God's wishes, so he tells the crew to throw him overboard to save themselves and the ship.

The ship's crew were scared by what Jonah told them so they reluctantly threw Jonah off the ship. God sends a large fish which rescues Jonah by swallowing him and delivering him to Ninevah. At Ninevah he follows God's wish and tells the people and their rulers to repent and change. The people and their rulers repent and change their evil ways and the city is saved.

The story shows that God cares about every human being. It is never too late to repent and change. God does not want severe and harsh judgments, but rather wants righteous and meaningful change. The story also shows that God is universal and no one can escape God's wishes.

As the service of the day of Yom Kippur nears the end, the Neilah or closing service is chanted and recited by the cantor and the congregation. Just as the day is ending, it's as though the gates are closing on the opportunity we have been given for improvement and renewal and we pray to God that it is not too late for us to do better with our lives and have a good year.

At the end of the following evening service, the shofar is blown for the first and only time on Yom Kippur. The shofar note is steady and long (as long as the breath, of the person blowing it, lasts).

At the conclusion of the service we wish each other again a good and happy new year and go home to be with our friends and family and break the fast with a hopeful feeling for the coming year.

Theme

The emphasis on Rosh Hashanah and Yom Kippur is taking responsibility to do the best we can to apply our Jewish ideals to our daily lives and achieve the renewal, meaning and fulfillment that this can bring

Rosh Hashanah and Yom Kippur are holidays for self reflection. A time that is very personal as we think about our lives, our feelings and our relationships.

We all want health and success. We also want value and meaning for our lives as well as happiness for the ones we love and hope for a better world.

All year we have been busy living our lives. Now as we think back on the previous year, we may become concerned that we have not done everything that we should have done or become everything that we wanted to be. In spite of our best efforts we may not have accomplished our goals or even acted towards our best intentions.

We may be concerned about health or financial problems. We may be worrying about the problems of our family and friends. We may be concerned about the sad state of our communities, our country and the world. We may also have suffered the loss of someone very close and dear.

For in spite of ourselves, we may not always do our best. In spite of our best efforts, we may not always be successful. In spite of our desires, our family and friends may not be spared from suffering and spite of all our wishes the future may still pose concerns.

But today is like "creation". We have a chance to start anew. Even if we have grown weak, today can give us strength. Even if we have grown tired and weary, today can give us inspiration and even if we have lost the vision of our dreams, today can give us new hope.

We know our forefathers found inspiration and solace in the ways of righteousness, prayer and good deeds. They wrapped themselves in their dedication to Torah and their Jewish way of life.

This reaffirmed for them as it can for us a role in the process of creation, allowing us to know the power and greatness of the love that lies within us, giving us the ability to live our lives in a way that brings happiness to ourselves and others.

Therefore, with Penitence, Prayer and Righteous Deeds, let it be said that:

From indifference we rescued caring.

From despair we rescued hope.

From fear we rescued courage.

From hate and anger we rescued love.

With caring, hope, courage and love,
WE RESCUED LIFE.

Sukkot, Shemini Atzeret and Simchat Torah

Introduction

Five days after Yom Kippur (beginning on the 15th of the Jewish month of Tishri) comes the festival of Sukkot which lasts for nine days. Sukkot means booths or tabernacles and it reminds us of the time, as discussed on Passover, when our ancestors had to live in the desert after being freed from slavery and leaving Egypt.

To commemorate this time, the Bible tells us to dwell in booths or tabernacles seven days each year in remembrance of these difficulties. The eighth day of Sukkot is referred to as Shemini Atzeret and the ninth day as Simchat Torah.

Later Sukkot also became a time for celebrating and being grateful for the crop harvest which also occurred in Autumn at this time of year. In the Bible Sukkot is called: Hag Ha Sukkot, the Festival of Booths (or Tabernacles), and it is also called: Hag Ha –Asif, the Festival of Ingathering (of crops).

Sukkot became a time for gratitude and thanksgiving. It became a time to express thankfulness to God for the bounty of the harvest and a time of expressing gratitude to God that we were able to survive, grow and prosper and no longer had to live in the difficulties of the desert.

Our ancestors were delivered from slavery to freedom and later at Mount Sinai they were given the Torah and a way to live (our Jewish way of life) to maintain that freedom. But they had to stop thinking of themselves as slaves.

They no longer were slaves and they had to start taking responsibility for their lives.

They now had to put into to practice, and practice on a daily basis, the morality, ethics and inspiration of their Jewish way of life so that they could live together and take care of each other.

They also had to take responsibility for their sustenance, to take care of themselves, their families and the community, working hard on a daily basis to provide food, shelter and all of the things needed for their daily lives.

Finding themselves in a desert wilderness they had to deal with great adversity. However with God's help, in spite of their adversity, they were able to find the courage and will to go on, survive, grow and later prosper and on Sukkot they were fulfilled by their efforts and grateful to God for what they had achieved.

On the eighth day of Sukkot, also referred to as Shemini Atzeret (the Eighth Day of Solemn Assembly), we remember our loved ones and others who have passed away and express our love and gratitude for the benefit of having had their presence in our lives. We pray that God take care of them, and we say Memorial prayers (Yizkor) at the synagogue or temple.

At the synagogue or temple the custom is also followed of reciting the prayer (Geshem) our ancestors used to say, thousands of years ago, to ask for rain. Rain to them was necessary for crops, food and sustenance. It was a necessary item to enable them to sustain their lives. For us today this is symbolic of asking God to help us provide for all of the things necessary to sustain our lives and obtain a prosperous year. We pray to God for these things and are grateful for all that we have achieved.

The ninth day of Sukkot is called Simchat Torah. Each week during the year a part of the Torah (Five Books of Moses) has been read in the services at the synagogue or temple.

On Simchat Torah the reading of the Torah is completed and will start all over again for the following year. On this day completing reading the Torah is celebrated as a truly great accomplishment.

The Torah is the basis for our Jewish way of life. It is God's gift to us as the basis for how we should live, how we should take care of ourselves, take care of each other and live together with righteous and loving behavior. Through the year we read and interpret the Torah on an on-going basis for application to our daily life.

Just as earlier in Sukkot we gave thanks for all that we had received during the year, on Simhat Torah we celebrate and give thanks for having been given the gift of Torah and the benefit of being able to read, study and apply it to our daily lives.

Celebration

After Yom Kippur the family participates in the construction of a simple booth or Sukkah which is put outside the main residence. It is made of simple boards, leaves and branches and is covered on top with separate leaves, twigs or straw instead of boards, so that the sky can be seen. Traditionally the family can decorate the inside with flowers, grapes, apples, pomegranates, and Indian corn.

At the beginning of Sukkot, a table is set in the Sukkah, and over the next seven days meals are eaten and prayers are made in the Sukkah during the festival. It's a wonderful time for the whole family to eat together outdoors in the Sukkah and reminisce on the past when things were more difficult and give thanks for what we have today.

As commanded in the Bible, and in accordance with tradition, in the Sukkah there are four things that are symbolic of and were used to show appreciation for, the bounty of the harvest. These are the etrog, the lulav, myrtle branches and willows of the brook.

The etrog is a citron fruit, it should be yellow and fragrant. The lulav is a sheath of palm fronds fastened with myrtle and willow twigs.

Over the years, there have been many discussions and explanations as to why these particular items were chosen to be used as part of our celebration.

The essence of most explanations is that these items were chosen to represent the diversity of things found in nature (appearance - color, size and shape, capabilities, other characteristics, etc.) which also represents the diversity and differences found in humanity and each individual.

However under God, all things and all people are unified. With righteous behavior, as taught by our tradition, diversity becomes a strength not a weakness. We can all work together, each with our own strengths and weaknesses making contributions in our own way.

So on Sukkot we are grateful to God for the bounty of what we have harvested and achieved during the year and we are also grateful to God for giving us a way to work together to better achieve and enhance our bounty.

Every morning during the first seven days of Sukkot (except on the Sabbath) a blessing is recited while standing in the Sukkah and holding the lulav in the right hand and the etrog in the left hand with the part that was attached to the stem pointing up. After the blessing, the etrog is held upside down and placed together with the lulav and waived together as one making the lulav rustle (Ref. 2).

At the temple or synagogue, in addition to the regular service, a special procession is held on each of the first seven days of Sukkot in which the Ark is opened and the cantor and rabbi are followed by everyone holding an etrog and lulav, while the cantor chants the Hoshanah prayer.

As discussed above, the eighth day of Sukkot is celebrated as Shemini Atzeret and the ninth day of Sukkot as Simhat Torah. On Shemini Atzeret the Yizkor (memorial) and Geshem services are recited at the temple or synagogue.

On the ninth day, Simhat Torah is celebrated as a very happy holiday. Traditionally the whole family comes to the temple or synagogue. Children can carry flags, fruit or candy. The congregation is fully given a chance to participate in reciting the blessing over reading the Torah including children under 13 who can recite a blessing together while covered by a large tallit spread over their heads.

All of the Torah Scrolls are taken out of the Ark and are carried around in a procession. Children and adults follow (singing, dancing, children carrying their flags). The sanctuary is circled seven times. At the end of the service refreshments are served.

As our ancestors had to do when they stopped being slaves, we have had to take responsibility and take charge of our lives.

All year we have had to work hard to provide for the things that we need and overcome any problems and adversity.

On Sukkot we express our gratitude to God for helping us do this. We thank God for all of our blessings and for the benefits of the gift of Torah and our Jewish way of life.

Theme

On Sukkot we remember a more humble time when our ancestors, newly delivered by God from slavery (as discussed on Passover), found themselves, full of doubts living in a desert wilderness.

At first the people still thought of themselves as slaves. They had not been used to taking care of themselves. Life in the wilderness was difficult and severe and they lacked the courage to take care of themselves and be free.

They had been slaves and did not know what it meant to be free. To be free meant that they now had to take care of themselves and take responsibility for everything that they did.

With God's help they were able, based on our Jewish righteous way of life, to find the courage and inspiration to be free and overcome their adversity and eventually prosper.

On Sukkot we sit in the Sukkah, outside, from where we normally live. In this humble surrounding, as we recite the blessings, we can look up at the sky and better appreciate the world around us, marvel at its vastness and beauty and feel closer to nature and God.

In this unpretentious setting we remember the humble circumstances and adversity that our forefathers endured and were able to overcome and we understand what is really basic and important in our lives.

Now we also accept that same responsibility to do our best to take care of ourselves, our families, our friends and our community.

We thank God for all of our blessings, for the benefits of the gift of Torah and our Jewish righteous way of life and we thank God and pray for all that we might still be able to do and achieve.

Hanukkah

Introduction

Before we know it, it is December and Hanukkah has arrived. Even though it is the beginning of winter, we feel happy and cheerful and look forward to celebrating with family and friends, sending out greeting cards, putting up decorations, lighting the menorah, exchanging gifts, eating good foods, having parties, singing songs, playing games and generally having a good time.

Hanukkah means dedication, and Hanukkah makes us feel good because it celebrates our dedication to our Jewish beliefs and ideals. Ideals which include the belief in a universal God that is good and just, that all human life is sanctified, that every person's life has meaning and value and every person can reach their full potential for loving, caring and achieving fulfillment and doing their best to making things better for themselves and others.

Going back almost 2200 hundred years (to 165 B.C.E.), Hanukkah starts on the 25th day of the Jewish month of Kislev (occurring during December) and lasts eight days. The first candle on the menorah is lit on the evening before.

Hanukkah officially started with the rededication of the Holy Temple in Jerusalem in 165 B.C.E. This occurred only after winning a hard and bitter struggle against a very powerful empire whose leader wanted to suppress our Jewish beliefs and religion because he wanted everyone to believe that he was like God, with complete life and death control over each person and every thing.

But this ran against all that we believe, and so we had to stand up for our beliefs and defend and fight to preserve these beliefs and our right to continue to practice them.

This was not the first time and it was not the last time that this has happened.

Many times in history and even today, attempts are made to treat people as commodities, to be used and discarded, solely for economic or political gain and we have had to try hard to preserve and defend our beliefs and values.

This was the case in 175 B.C.E. when Antiochus Epiphanes ("the glorious") became king of the portion of the empire, established earlier by Alexander the Great, that included the Jewish country (approximately in the area of Israel) and it's capital Jerusalem.

Antiochus wanted to control everyone to the point where he wanted everyone to believe that he was God. He hated the Jewish people because they remained faithful to their own religion and did not accept worship of him or any other idols.

He tried to destroy the Jewish ideals and religion. He issued orders forbidding Jewish practice and observance. He desecrated the Holy Temple in Jerusalem. He tried, in every other way that he could, to intimidate, demoralize and stop Jewish practice and belief.

In response to this terrible time Mattathias, of the Hasmonean family in the small village of Modi'in, and his five sons Judah Maccabee, Jonathan, Johanan, Eleazer and Simon lead a revolt against Antiochus and his armies.

There was a long and bitter struggle in which many suffered and died. However, lead by Judah Maccabee they were finally victorious and on the twenty-fifth day of Kislev in 165 B.C.E. the Holy Temple in Jerusalem was rededicated to serve the Jewish community.

When they rededicated the Temple they searched for the special holy oil required to relight the Great Menorah. All they could find, which had not been destroyed, was a little flask. With only the small amount of oil left, they re-lit the Great Menorah.

To everyone's great surprise and delight instead of just burning a short time, the oil miraculously lasted eight days.

To commemorate the great victory won against all odds, the subsequent rededication to our Jewish ideals, the resulting renewal of hope and inspiration as further symbolized by the light of the Menorah shinning for eight days, miraculously much longer and stronger than ever expected, Hanukkah as a holiday was established and has been celebrated as a holiday for eight days from that time (and the Menorah used for Hanukah was made to have eight branches instead of the seven branched Menorah used in the temple).

Hanukkah is also referred to as the festival of lights referring to the lighting of the Menorah which is symbolic of the light that dedication to our Jewish ideals and righteous way of life brings to our lives.

Celebration

Hanukkah is a very festive time. It is a very happy holiday. It is a time for enjoyment and good memories, a time to be together with family and friends and it is a time to appreciate each other and the spirit of life, love and hope that dedication to our Jewish ideals and way of life brings.

Celebration starts on the first evening of Hanukkah, with the lighting of the first candle on the Menorah. Traditionally because the Hanukkah candles can't be used for illumination or to light each other, the ninth candle (usually in the middle or on the end) which is the shammash (helper), is used to light the other candles.

An additional candle is lit each night (one the first night, two the second, three the third, etc.) until a total of eight candles (plus the shammash) are lit on the eighth night (Traditionally the first candle is put in at the right of the Menorah, with each new candle placed to the left of the previous ones. Candles are lit starting with the left most candle and then lighting the candles moving to the right.).

On each night as candles are lit on the Menorah, blessings are made, songs are sung and celebration continues through the holiday.

Before the candles are lit, the following blessing is recited:

"Ba-ruch A-ta Adonni, E-lo-hey-nu Me-lech ha-o-lam a-sher ki-d'-sha-nu b'mitz-vo-tav v'tzi-vanu l'hadlik ner shel Hanukkah (English pronunciation of the Hebrew version of the prayer)."

"Blessed are you, Lord our God, King of the universe, who has sanctified us through your commandments and who has commanded us to light the candles on Hanukkah."

Also recited is the blessing:

"Blessed are you, Lord our God, King of the universe, who wrought miracles for our forefathers, at this season. "

 On the first night, the following blessing is also recited before lighting the first candle:

46

"Blessed are you, Lord our God, King of the universe, who has kept us alive, sustained us, and brought us to this season."

In many homes, additional blessings and personal prayers are also recited.

Starting before and continuing through the holiday, people send each other greeting cards, exchange gifts, put up decorations, have parties, eat good food, sing songs, play games and celebrate at home, at work, and celebrate with the congregation at temple or synagogue.

There are many interesting and wonderful books and Internet websites that present discussions and information on ways to enjoy and celebrate Hanukkah, including songs and music, food and recipes, games, decorations, gifts, greeting cards etc. Some of these are included in the Appendix. The idea is to make the Holiday a positive and memorable experience.

There are many songs that are popular for Hanukkah. Some of these include, Rock of Ages (Ma-0z Tzur) and Hanerot Halalu. These and many other songs are available at the web sites discussed further in the Appendix.

There are many popular Hanukkah foods. One of the most well known are latkes (potato pancakes). They can be made in many different ways. There are of course many interesting recipes and foods available for the holidays, some of these are discussed at the web sites presented in the Appendix. Hanukkah is celebrated at home, but parties and celebrations can take place anywhere.

At the temple or synagogue there are no special services, but at the evening service candles are lit just as at home and services during the holiday contain some additional prayers.

In addition to the Hanukkah Menorah, a popular symbol of the holiday is the dreidel which is a four sided top which has one of four Hebrew letters Nun, Gimel, Hay, Shin on each side. These initials stand for Nes, Gadol, Hayah, Sham which means a great miracle happened there.

The legend is that the dreidel was developed at the time of the Maccabees.

The people were forbidden to study Torah so they would gather in groups and study in secret.

The dreidel was put on the table. If soldiers approached, the students would pretend that they were spinning the top and playing an innocent game using the dreidel, thus saving many lives and allowing study to continue.

Since that time dreidels and dreidel games have become part of Hanukkah and its celebration.

Spin the dreidel and see how you have done. Nun, and you win nothing from the pot. Gimel and you win the whole pot. Hay wins half the pot and with shin you have to add to the pot.

Theme

Hanukkah is a happy holiday.
We light candles, eat tasty foods, play games and sing songs.
There is a festive mood.
We give each other presents and enjoy
the close company of family and friends.
These things give us pleasure and
a feeling of self value.

However, it hasn't always been like this.

Throughout history there have been times when people were abused and oppressed. Individual rights were ignored, thoughts and beliefs were surpressed and people were demeaned as human beings.

Our forefathers knew that this was wrong.
People were not merely objects to be used and controlled,
economic and political commodities,
to be deprived of meaningfulness and
to be consumed and thrown away.

Our forefathers knew that God's gift
was the sanctity of human life.
With God's help they developed our Jewish way of life,
dedicated to honoring and achieving this sanctity in every thing that
we do.

Their goal was a world in which life is sacred.
A world with love and peace.
A world in which each person can hope for and achieve
fulfillment and happiness.

On Hanukah we celebrate a great victory.
A victory at the time of the Maccabees,
who as a small band struggled against a mighty empire.
They fought many battles,
each against insurmountable odds.
They endured great hardships and many died.
Yet they were willing to fight for what they believed
and in the end they won.

We are grateful to them and all who came before and all who followed, who have given us what we have today.

And to commemorate this appreciation and gratitude,

we light the menorah,
whose light gives us inspiration and hope,
and whose light reminds us of the great light that our Jewish Ideals,
give to our lives.

So as we light the menorah,
just for a moment,
our hearts flicker as the candles, with the hearts of the Maccabees,
and we have the courage and strength to stand up for and live our
Jewish Ideals.

Ideals which provide a way of life that gives us self respect,
compassion, and love for others,
a way of life that gives us meaning and value.

A way of life that gives us pride in what we are,
pride in what we have been,
and hope for what we still can do.

Tu Bi-Shevat (Hamishah Asar Bi-Shevat)

Introduction

Historically our ancestors lived, in Israel, in an agricultural society and celebrated and observed the beginning and ending of different seasons as it affected and impacted the planting and harvesting of their crops and plants which they used for sustenance and making their living. In previous sections, it was discussed how these seasonal issues of planting and harvesting influenced the celebration of several of our other holidays (e.g., Passover, Shavuot, and Sukkot).

Tu Bi-Shevat, occurring on the fifteenth day of the Jewish month of Shevat, (approximately the beginning of February or end of January) came in Israel toward the end of winter, and was set aside by our ancestors to celebrate the renewal, re-greening and blossoming of their trees. This renewal, was an important indication that once again the winter would end, spring would come, crops could be planted and life could go on.

Trees also were an important part of their agriculture environment contributing to shade, irrigation, soil fertility, food and building products, and the beauty and appearance of the land and, for them, symbolized the importance and beauty of nature and strength and enduring life.

Our ancestors knew the importance of taking care of the world and natural environment within which they lived and they incorporated these concepts into our Jewish Heritage and way of life. They knew that part of righteous behavior is for us to take responsibility to do the best we can to enhance and take care of our world as well as taking care of ourselves and each other.

On Tu Bi-Shevat also, referred to as "The New Year of the Trees" (" Rosh Hashanah Lailanot"), we celebrate and give thanks to God for the blessing of our natural world, the trees, plants, lands, etc. and reaffirm our responsibility to do the best we can to appropriately take care of, protect and enhance the natural environment and world within which we live.

Celebration

At the temple or synagogue prayers are recited expressing to God our gratitude for the continued blessing of our plants, trees and natural environment which provide us with food, beauty, products, fresh air and other sustenance.

Celebration emphasizes outdoor activities, with outings, picnics and hikes. In many cases young trees or other plants are planted to commemorate the holiday. At home and at school, fruits and vegetables are served and young trees or plants may be planted outside in the garden. As in all festivals good music and food are enjoyed as part of the celebration.

Theme

On Tu Bi-Shivat, we are reminded of the importance, and thank God for the blessing of, our natural environment including the plants, trees, fields, open spaces, nature and the world within which we live. We celebrate these things and we acknowledge our own responsibility to help take care of, enhance and preserve them to help insure their current and future availability, enjoyment and use, for all of us.

So as we celebrate by planting new trees and plants out-side, we think of the time when winter will start to ebb. The sun will seem to shine with a warmer glow and we will see the flowers and leaves on plants and trees starting to bloom and grow.

We will feel cheerful and filled with hope. Everywhere we look we will see renewal and new growth. Once again we will be able to look forward to the coming of spring and summer and the bounty and beauty of life that this will bring.

We thank God for this blessing and we know, as our ancestors did, that we must take responsibility and do everything that we can to insure that this will continue again, and again, with each year, every year.

Purim

Introduction

The Megillah, the Scroll of Esther (in the Writings portion of the Bible) which is read in the temple or synagogue on the 14th day of the Hebrew month of Adar (approximately the end of February or to the middle of March) tells us to keep that day as a day of joy and happiness, which we celebrate as the holiday of Purim.

The Megillah tells the story of how years ago the Persian Empire included many of the areas where Jewish people lived (including Israel, Persia, and many other areas ranging from Ethiopia to India). King Ahasuerus was the ruler at that time.

King Ahasuerus ordered a feast in Shushan, his capital. He invited all the princes and governors from his provinces to the feast. The feast went on for seven days where he displayed the riches of his empire and ate and drank with his guests.

At some point in the feasting the king under the influence of the heavy drinking started boasting that everything he had was the best in the world, better than anyone else's. His horses were the best, as were his jewels, his gardens, etc.

Upon being questioned about his queen, King Ahasuerus boasted that Queen Vashti, his queen, was the most beautiful woman in the world and he ordered her to appear at once, without proper dress or preparation, to prove his boast to the other princes.

The queen was insulted by the degrading circumstances and purpose of the request and refused to appear. The king was embarrassed in front of the other princes whom he was trying to impress and he became infuriated, ordering the queen to leave the palace and the kingdom.

After that, King Ahasuerus realized that he was now very lonely.

He issued a proclamation that all of the fairest maidens of the land were to gather before him and the one he found most pleasing would be made queen in place of Vashti.

A large number of contestants applied and paraded before the king for his approval.

One of these was Esther (Hadassah), a Jewish girl, who had been adopted by Mordecai (Esther was his uncles daughter), as his own daughter after her father and mother had died.

When Esther appeared before the king he loved her more than all the other women and he made her queen instead of Vashti.

One day while Mordecai was sitting in the king's gate to the palace, two of the king's servants, who guarded the entrance, plotted to kill King Ahasuerus.

Mordecai learned of the plot and told Queen Esther. She told it to the king in Mordecai's name and the plot was thwarted. The incident was recorded in the daily record of events that was kept for the king.

At that time, King Ahasuerus promoted one of his officials, Haman, to a high position above other princes and the king's servants who were at the king's gate were commanded to bow down to Haman.

But Mordecai, as a Jew, felt he could not bow down as Haman wanted.

Haman was very angry and decided to plot to destroy Mordecai and the other Jews in the kingdom.

Haman told King Ahasuerus, that there was a certain people in his kingdom that had different laws than every other people and they did not keep the king's laws. Haman asked the king for an order to destroy them and Haman said he would pay ten thousand talents of silver into the king's treasury.

The king gave Haman the king's ring and the king told Haman that Haman could do what he wanted with the people.

An order and messages were sent to the king's provinces to destroy all of the Jews on the thirteenth day of the twelfth month which is Adar.

Mordeci found out about the order and wanted Esther to go right away and plead with the king to save her people.

Esther was concerned that death was the punishment for any person who went to see the king without first being called unless the king held out his scepter and agreed to see them and Esther had not been called to go to the king for thirty days.

Mordecai told Esther that if the order was carried out she as a Jew would also be included and she would not be sparred. If she did nothing, help would come from somewhere else, but this was her chance to use her unique position as queen to try to save her people.

Esther asked Mordecai to gather all the Jews in Shushan and have them fast for her. She asked them not to eat or drink anything for three days and nights and she and her servants would also fast.

She would then go to the king, although it was against the law, and risk the possibility that she might perish. Mordecai did as Esther directed.

On the third day Esther wearing her royal robs went, without first being asked, to see the king in his inner court. The king then held out his royal scepter and said to her:

"Whatever you wish, Queen Esther, and whatever you ask, it shall be granted even to the half of my kingdom." (Ref. 2, page 49) Esther then asked that the king and Haman come that day to the feast which she had prepared for them.

The king and Haman came to the feast which Esther had prepared and she then invited them to come to another feast the next day.

Haman left happy that day but became infuriated when he saw Mordecai (who would not bow) at the king's gate.

Haman told his friends and his wife, Zeresh, that even though Esther had invited only him with the king that day and the next day, he could not be satisfied as long as he had to see Mordecai at the King's gate.

His friends and his wife advised Haman that he should have a gallows built and in the morning speak to the king and have Mordecai executed. Haman accepted the advice and had the gallows built.

That evening the king was not able to sleep. He gave orders to his servants to read for him from the books where great deeds had been recorded.

Among the things read was the record of how Mordecai had uncovered the plot to kill the king. The king asked how Mordecai had been honored and rewarded for this and the king was told nothing had been done.

Just at that time Haman happen to come to speak to the king about the gallows Haman had built and Haman's plan to deal with Mordecai.

When Haman entered, the king asked "What shall be done to the man whom the king delights to honor?" (Ref. 2)

Haman thought the king meant him (Haman) and said: "Let a royal garment be brought, which the king has worn, and the horse on which the king has ridden and whose head a royal crown has been placed. Then let the garment and the horse be placed in charge of one of the king's noble princes and let him clothe the man whom the king delights to honor and make him ride on the horse through the city square and proclaim before him: 'This is what is done to the man whom the king delights to honor."(Ref. 2)

The king then told Haman to take the garment and the horse and do what Haman had said, for Mordecai. Haman obeyed the king and did what was said for Mordecai and then went home very upset. Later Haman went to the feast that Esther had prepared.

At the feast while Haman and the King where drinking with Queen Esther, the king again said: "Whatever you ask, Queen Esther, it shall be granted to you, even to the half of my kingdom."

Queen Esther answered: "If I have won favor, O king, and if it seems best to the king, let my life and my people be given me at my request; for I and my people have been sold to be destroyed, to be killed, and to perish!"

The King asked Esther: "Who is he and where is he who dares to do this?" Esther answered: "A foe, an enemy, this wicked Haman." (Ref. 2, page 50)

Haman was hanged on the gallows that Haman had prepared for Mordecai.

The king made Mordecai one of his advisors and gave him authority to stop the destruction of the Jews. Messengers where sent to every city to warn the Jews to gather together and protect themselves and to relay the King's command to stop any planned destruction of the Jews.

Mordecai also told the Jews to keep the 14th day of the month of Adar as a holiday. What could have been a time of great sorrow and catastrophe instead became a time of gladness and celebration.

On this day the Jews rested and rejoiced and it became the day that we celebrate Purim. The Jews in Shushan rested on the 15th day of Adar and made it the day of feasting and rejoicing.

Purim means lots (lots means a way of using some type of objects for deciding something by chance, such as drawing cards, drawing straws, flipping coins, etc.) for Haman cast lots to decide on the best time to send his forces against the Jews, but Haman's plan was of course thwarted as described above.

Celebration

Purim is celebrated at home, at work, in the community and at the temple or synagogue and with special foods, meals and get-togethers with family and friends, parties, masquerade parties, plays and carnivals.

The Purim play in which all of the characters and the story are depicted, as told in the Megillah (portion of the Torah), and Purim carnivals have became part of the standard tradition of Purim.

Hamantashen are three- cornered pastry cakes filled with poppy-seeds or plum jam which are traditionally eaten on Purim. One legend is that the cakes resemble Haman's hat.

A gragger is the name of the noisemaker used to make a noise every time the name of Haman is mentioned when reading the Scroll of Esther (Megillah) the same thing is done during the Purim play.

Mishloah Manot (Shalach Monos) refers to the custom of giving and receiving gifts on Purim, which dates back to the Megillah itself which states :
 "make them days of feasting and joy, of sending portions to one another." (Ref. 2)

The day before Purim (13th of Adar) is the Fast of Esther to commemorate the fast and prayer decreed by Esther for herself and the Jewish people before she went to the king to stop Haman's plot.

The day after Purim is called Shushan Purim which was celebrated in Shushan, the capital of King Ahasuerus' empire, because the Jews in Shushan s were still in battle, according to the Book of Esther, and ended up celebrating a day later.

60

The Book (or Megillah or Scroll) of Esther is in the third part of the Holy Scriptures (in the Ketuvim, or Writings). It is read in the synagogue or temple after the evening service on the evening before the day of Purim (Eve of Purim) and again on the morning of the day of Purim. Machatzit Hashekel refers to the custom of contributing to charity before the Scroll is read in remembrance of the biblical tax which was paid to maintain the Holy Sanctuary.

Theme

We celebrate Purim and are happy today because we were saved from a great catastrophe; a catastrophe which could have destroyed our entire people. But instead of grief and sorrow, we feel cheerful and full of fun.

We play games, eat Hamantashen and retell the story of Purim. The story of how a young girl, Esther, rises from being an orphan to become queen and then risks everything, her high position and all she has up to and including her very life, to try to save her family and her people.

How Mordecai, doing what he thought was right, first saves Esther from being an orphan, then saves the king from assassination and in the end saves his people from destruction.

How King Ahasuerus, though vain and vengeful at first, later finds love for his queen and as a result is willing to give her up to half of his kingdom and save a nation.

How our people were able to ban together and successfully defend themselves and how Haman though powerful and full of hate was defeated by the caring and righteous actions of the very people he has trying to destroy.

In every generation tyrants have risen up bent on hatred and destruction, but the lesson of Purim, which we have learned many times, is that when we all care for each other these tyrants can be defeated.

Had Mordecai not cared for Esther, had Esther not cared for Mordecai, had neither cared about their people, had King Ahasuerus not cared about Esther, had our people not cared about each other, all would have been lost.

In the end, instead of being destroyed by indifference, anger and hate,
we were saved by caring, compassion and love.

So let us celebrate Purim today and the lessions that it teaches us.
Let us always honor, care for and protect each other
and let us celebrate the joy, strength, happiness and fulfillment
that this can bring.

Tishah Be-Av, Yom Ha-Shoah, and Yom Ha-Atzma-ut

There are several events in Jewish History that are commemorated in addition to the holidays already discussed.

Tishah Be-Av

Tishah Be-Av, occurring on the 9th day of the Hebrew Month of Av, (approximately mid-July beginning of August), remembers the destruction, by outside conquerors, of the First Temple over 2500 years ago (in 586 B.C.E.) and the destruction over 600 years later (in 70 C.E.) of the subsequently rebuilt Second Temple. Commemoration services are held in the temple or synagogue and on an individual basis there is a fast. Fasting is not for punishment, but rather to show the strength of our resolve and concern whenever our Jewish righteous ideals and way of life are threatened.

Living in Israel, our ancestors used the Temple (first and second) located in Jerusalem, as the central place of worship. It was the center of religious practice, religious thought and authority. It was very terrible, difficult and sad, when the temple was destroyed each time by outside conquerors.

At first in each case the people did not know what to do. The center of their support and religious practice had been destroyed.

But in each case the people showed that Judaism and their religious practice could go on. It wasn't in a building or a place, but rather in each person and their relationship with God. Responsibility for maintaining their Jewish way of life shifted to each individual and the local communities within which they lived.

When the temples were destroyed, it was an attempt to destroy our Jewish ideals and way of life. It did not succeed. Since then there have been many attempts to subdue and destroy these ideals which also have not succeeded. Miraculously, over thousands of years, our Jewish ideals and practice have been kept alive for our use and benefit today, and we thank God for this wonderful gift.

Yom Ha-Shoah

Occurring on the 27th day of the Hebrew month of Nissan (end of April beginning of May) Yom Hashoah commemorates a very difficult time in Jewish History referred to as the Holocaust, during a period starting in the 1930's and ending in 1945, when millions of Jewish people were imprisoned, enslaved and murdered solely because they were Jewish. It was a terrible time in Jewish and world history which was not ended until the defeat of Nazi Germany in World War II in 1945.

On Yom Ha-Shoah, memorial services are held at the temple or synagogue for the lives lost and memorial candles are lit at home. The theme of the day is to remember those lives lost and to reaffirm our principles of righteous behavior and our resolve to do whatever we can to insure that this type of thing will never happen again.

Besides the Jewish people killed, there were millions of other people killed during this period because of oppression, the denial of basic human rights, and the fighting and destruction that took place in the resultant war.

Because of anger, hate, intolerance, and the denial of basic human rights, the world paid a terrible price in terms of suffering, death and destruction.

We therefore pray to God that this type of thing will never happen again. We thank God for the gift of our righteous ideals and reaffirm our responsibility to apply these whenever we can.

We pray that the whole world will learn the lesson that we must all be able to live together, to work together, to live in tolerance of each other, to respect each other, to honor the sanctity of human life and to apply these basic principles to taking care of ourselves and each other.

We thank God for the chance to apply these concepts in our own lives, to apply these concepts with each other, to apply these concepts in our communities and to help support the application of these concepts in the rest of the world.

Yom Ha-Atzma-ut

Dating back to May 14, 1948 when the current State of Israel was established, Yom ha-Atzma-ut, Israel Independence Day, is celebrated on the 5th day of the Hebrew month of Iyar (approximately April, beginning of May). For over three thousand years, since the time of the Bible, Jewish people have lived in and been associated with Israel.

Israel is the place where much of the Bible takes place, it is the place where basic Jewish ideas and ideals were developed and Israel has always been associated with and played an important part in Jewish History.

Today Israel has over approximately 5.7 million Jews and over approximately 1.9 million Moslems, Christians and people of other religions and faiths and is an important center for Jewish religious thought and culture.

Israel Independence Day is remembered with commemorative services, picnics, outings, and get-togethers.

Appendix

The Jewish Calendar

The Internet As An Additional Source of Holiday Information (Food, Songs/Music, And Ways To Celebrate)

Appendix

The Jewish Calendar

In the Jewish calendar, the day begins at sunset. So for example, the Sabbath, the seventh day of the week, begins on Friday evening at sunset and ends on Saturday at sunset. All holidays begin at sunset of the day before.

The Jewish calendar has 12 months. Months are lunar months with 29 or 30 days. However this creates a problem in keeping the calendar consistent with the seasons which correspond to the earth's rotation around the sun. For example, with an approximate average month length of 29 ½ days, in a 12 month year, there would only be 354 days in the year and the solar year would exceed this lunar year by over 11 days. To keep the calendar consistent with the seasons and the years which correspond to the earth's rotation around the sun, an extra month is added to the calendar seven times every nineteen years.

The extra month is added after the month of Adar and is called Adar Sheni (Second Adar). The extra month (Adar Sheni) is added every third, sixth, eighth, eleventh, fourteenth, seventeenth and nineteenth year.

The names of the 12 months are Nisan, Iyar, Sivan, Tammuz, Av, Elul, Tishri, Heshvan, Kislev, Tevet, Shevat and Adar.

A special blessing for the new month is made at the temple or synagogue on the Sabbath before the beginning of the month where we ask that we be granted a month of good health and happiness. On the first day (Rosh Hodesh) of the new month, prayers of thanksgiving are read at services at the temple or synagogue.

The following is a listing of the start dates (all holidays start after sundown on the evening before) of the holidays discussed.

Holiday	Hebrew Calendar Start Date	Approximate Corresponding Time of Year
Sabbath	7[Th] day of week (Saturday)	Every week of the year
Passover	15th of Nisan	End of March, April
Yom Ha-Shoah	27th of Niasn	End of April, beginning of May
Yom Ha-Atzma-ut	5th of Iyar	April, May
Shavuot	6th of Sivan	Mid-May, beginning of June
Tishah Be-Av	9th of Av	Mid- July, beginning of August
Rosh Hashanah And Yom Kippur	1st of Tishri 10th of Tishri	September September, beginning of October
Sukkot, Shemini Atzeret and Simchat Torah	15th of Tishri	End of September, October

Hunukkah	25th of Kislev	December
Tu Bi-Shevat	15th of Shevat	End of January, beginning of February
Purim	14th of Adar	End of February, beginning of March

The Internet as an Additional Source of Holiday Information (Food, Songs/Music, and Ways to Celebrate)

Nowadays there is a lot of material on the Internet which can be useful in helping to get good ideas and ways to help improve and support celebration of the holidays. The major Jewish denominations (including Orthodox, Conservative, and Reform) have web sites. Many individual congregations have web sites. Many Jewish organizations have web sites and many consumer oriented merchants and stores have web sites providing books and products to help in celebrating each holiday.

To tap this resource, one merely has to do a search on "Jewish Holidays", "Jewish Holidays, music", "Jewish Holidays, food", etc. and a large number of sites will be obtained that can be selectively reviewed based on individual interest, taste and need.

Example Web Sites

There are of course a large number of organizational, educational, and commercial web sites which provide information and sell products to help enhance holiday observance and celebration.

We strongly encourage each reader to fully explore this cornucopia of web information and discover for themselves what is most appropriate for their own tastes and needs. To help begin this exploration, the following provides examples of several interesting web sites.

www.ou.org

This is the web site for The Orthodox Union (OU). The OU site provides religious and educational information and information on synagogues, publications and cultural issues, for Orthodox Jewry.

www.uscj.org

This is the web site for The United Synagogue of Conservative Judaism (USCJ), which supports conservative congregations in North America.

www.urj.org

This is the web site for the Union for Reform Judaism (URJ) which was previously named the Union of American Hebrew Congregations (UAHC). URJ supports Reform Jewish congregations in North America.

www.jewishrecipes.org

This is an example web site providing a wide selection of typical Jewish recipes and food.

www.jewishmusic.com

An example commercial web site providing a wide selection of music books, sheet music, recordings and videos for Jewish Music for purchase over the Internet.

References

1. Encyclopaedia Judaica, Volume 14, Page 558, Ketter Publishing House Ltd,1971

2. All About Jewish Holidays and Customs, Morris Epstein, KTAV Publishing House Inc., 1970

3. The Passover Haggadah, Rabbi Morris Silverman, The Prayer Book Press, Media Judaica Inc., 1978

4. High Holiday Prayer Book, Compiled and arranged by Rabbi Morris Silverman, The Prayer Book Press, Media Judaica Inc., 1978

5. The Concise Guide To Judaism, Rabbi Roy A. Rosenbeg, A Meridian Book,1994

6. The Jewish Festivals, Hayyim Schauss, Translated by Sammuel Jaffe, Union Of American Hebrew Congregations, 1938